"*Paganism For Kiddos* is a comprehensive and unique resource for school-aged children and their parents to learn about modern Paganism while affirming the validity of all religious paths. I would highly recommend it not only for Pagan families, but also for those who aren't Pagan but want to know more. Jessica Hauptmann has found a way to share about modern Wiccan and Pagan beliefs and practices in a way that is understandable while fostering a questioning and exploratory attitude. She teaches with openness and warmth, and strikes the right balance between detail and simplicity. Meant to be read to younger children or for older children to read on their own and discuss with parents, this beautiful and heartfelt book opens the door to really important conversations and teachable moments between parents and children while leaving the very personal decisions of what to believe and do to families."

-Joy Burton, M.S.Ed.

Joy is a wife and mother of three children. An eclectic Wiccan for over 20 years, she is the executive director and high priestess of Living Earth, a Pagan open circle and church of over 800 members in the South Denver area, and the internationally-known Pagan Beltane festival, Beltania. www.livingearthcolorado.org

"Jessica Hauptmann has created a gorgeous and heartfelt new classic for young people drawn to earth-based spirituality. I can imagine myself curled up with my grandson one winter day drinking hot chocolate reading this aloud together... This will be helpful for Pagan adults to explain their path to their kids, a great "text" to use in child care/children's groups at Pagan festivals and encampments, a great tool of teaching about spiritual diversity for school teachers, and a gift to young people seeking their own path. She heads straight for the heart-essence of ritual and for deep care and commitment to the natural world in her explanations. Her book is a valuable contribution to the re-emerging earth-based movement."

- Anne Z. Parker, Ph.D., author of *Stories from the Origin* and *Earth Alchemy*.

Paganism for Kiddos:

A Kids and Parents' Guide to Pagan and Wiccan Practice

Spiral Tree Publishing

Spiral Tree Publishing

Photography by Jessica N. and Jessica M. Hauptmann. Other photography not by author is credited in Acknowledgements.

ISBN-10: 0988825015
ISBN-13: 978-0-9888250-1-7

To the little peeps, innocent and curious, for
in their evolution lies a promise to the future.

What's Inside...

Foreword

When I was young I preferred to play alone than with kids from the neighborhood. I brought my Barbie dolls and Fisher-Price toys outside and played on the grass near trees, bushes, and gardens. Even in a sixteenth-floor apartment I played near the potted plants on the balcony and enjoyed the warm Caribbean breeze. I have always felt an affinity with nature, and while I am not a devout animal activist, I do help out the little creatures that travel past my yard. I discovered Wicca in my early thirties, or perhaps Wicca discovered me. Through my studies of the Craft I began to understand the connection I had always felt with the Moon and the Sun. I noticed that all along I have lived my years in relation to the seasons; the transformation going on outside was also happening within my being. The cycle of the seasons brings new plants and new life outdoors, for me it brings new life experiences, lessons, and memories.

I studied and practiced Wicca for two years through self-study, ritual gatherings, and with the help of a mentor. I called myself an eclectic solitary and did not commit to a specific Wiccan tradition. After this period I dabbled in Buddhism and Hinduism but my heart turned my attention back to Paganism. Since then I have continued a Pagan path and I will always be fond of the Wiccan practices which led me to the nature-centered path I walk today.

I played with the idea of writing a children's book for about a year. Finally, the opportunity to begin came to light after learning that I could write a book for a project in graduate school. Many of the Pagan and Wiccan books published are meant for an adult or young adult audience. I have not found a book that teaches the foundations or basics of Paganism and Wicca with children as the focus. Perhaps there are children books out there but not with the vision I intended.

For the child in a Pagan family, or in a different tradition, this book spells out the "whats" in Paganism and in a less traditional Wicca. I wrote this book as a guide and an outline for Pagan and Wiccan parents to explain the fundamentals of these paths to their children; my views are just another way for the parents to use in their explanation to their child, if they wish. The book provides the kick-start, the parents resume with the lessons.

Teach your children well. Blessed be.

"It is better that you should leave than enter the circle with fear in your heart. How do you enter?...With perfect love and perfect trust."

-Gardnerian Initiation Rites

How to Use this Book

The chapters in this book are intended to explain the more popular aspects of Paganism, Eclectic Wicca, and the occult in the most basic way. A brief explanation and some examples are provided for each topic but do not go into deeper detail to encourage the young reader to do more of the research himself, and also to allow the parent reading along with his child to provide insight from his or the household's belief system. The chapters do not have to be read in order but they were written and listed in a way that builds from the previous. The chapters also progress from the most basic foundations of Paganism to more specific ones. The bold words found in each chapter are again defined in the glossary at the end of the book.

Paganism, like any religion, is a practice that can be uniquely molded by the individual to fit his personal needs and beliefs. The contents of this book are not a final say of what Paganism or Wicca is; it is simply the belief system of the author put into words to help others learn how these practices are defined from an insider's experiential point of view and not necessarily as textbook material. Religion *is* personal.

What is Religion?

"Religion" is a tricky word. The word religion has many definitions and these many definitions can also be to other words that are not the word "religion." Yes, it's tricky, but that's why it is such a special word. **Religion** is the way that we live and behave everyday by doing good things so that we become better people and develop a deeper connection with a special force that is outside ourselves, or within ourselves, or doesn't exist at all. There is no right or wrong religion.

Religion is special because it is unique to each individual. Even if you believe in the same religion as your mom or dad or sister, you each follow that same religion in a different way; it is special and unique to who you are. There are some other words that also mean the same thing as religion, like faith, practice, or path. Whatever path you choose to walk on, even if you choose no path, that is your special path. Each person in the world has his own unique practice, faith, religion, or path. Do you know how many people there are on the planet? 7 billion! That's how many paths there are, billions of paths! And they are all special.

What is Paganism?

Paganism is a term or a word that includes many religions. It's like saying the word "breakfast" and then naming some foods that fall in that category, like French toast, pancakes, or scrambled eggs. Paganism includes religions like indigenous religions, Dark-green religions, Druidism, and Wicca. A Pagan may follow a specific religion or he can just honor and love all aspects of nature. Most Pagans live as one with the seasons, the Moon and the Sun, the elements, the animals, and plants. People that follow Pagan religions sometimes believe in many gods and goddesses, or believe in only one god or one goddess, or do not believe in a god.

What ties Pagan religions together is their connection with **Nature** and their desire to protect Mother **Gaia**. The planet is our home and we must respect her and honor her. Do you like to stomp in puddles after a rainstorm? Do you like to help animals that are hurt, like a baby bird that fell out of his nest? Do you like to play with your toy cars or dolls outside in the bushes? These are all ways that you are also connected with nature!

Exercise: Go to your backyard and pick up a rock, or a flower, or a little bug. Say three things why it special to our planet and why it is special to you.

What is Wicca?

Wicca is considered a modern religion which was developed in the 1950s. Even though it is new, it includes many ancient teachings and practices from our ancestors. You can say that it is a new religion of the past. Many years ago, hundreds of years, the word *wicca* meant a "male witch." It also meant "wise" or the "wise ones." Today, Wicca can mean a witch and it can also mean the *Craft* which is the many things that make up the practice of Wicca. Wicca has so many words! To put these words together we can say that Wicca is the religion, witchcraft is the practice, and witch or Wiccan is the person.

Wiccan priests and priestesses are those who went through specific training for quite some time with the guidance of a qualified teacher. The traditional Wiccan view is that a student should work with a properly initiated teacher so that all lessons are covered and nothing is missed. There are other Wiccans who choose to study on their own and learn the practice by participating with their community. If Wicca is a path that interests you and while it is great to study at your own pace, you should consider seeking a highly trained and initiated Wiccan teacher to guide your studies and your personal growth in the right direction.

Types of Wicca

Remember how earlier we learned that Paganism is divided into different religions and Wicca is one of them? Well Wicca is also divided into other paths. Some of the many Wiccan paths are: Dianic Wicca which focuses mainly on the Goddess and feminine qualities and energies; Celtic Wicca which follows the Celtic gods, goddesses, elementals, fairies, and trees; and Eclectic Wicca which means that the person doesn't follow a specific Wiccan path and learns and borrows from other practices to make a path that works best for him. Some Wiccans practice in groups called **covens**, **circles**, or **open circles**, and some prefer to practice alone which is called a **solitary** practitioner. Remember, there is no right or wrong way to practice Wicca or any religion.

Magick and Witches

A witch is a person, a man or a woman, who practices witchcraft or magick. Magick with a "ck" is different than magic with a "c". **Magick** is a way to guide or direct energy towards things that we would like to change or things we need a little help with, like gathering good or positive energy to send out to the baby bird that fell out of the nest. Magic is when we see a magician on a stage doing magic tricks, like pulling a rabbit out of a hat or making things disappear. A **ritual** is when witches get together in celebration to honor the gods and make magick. "Going to ritual" is similar to saying "going to church or temple" for those in other religions. Two things to remember are that witches could be of other religions too, and that there are witches that don't use magick or do spells, they can just rely on Nature to help.

The Divine

Some Pagans believe that there is a **Divine** entity that created the cosmos, the heavens, and the Earth. This is similar to what other religions may call God. The Divine can have several names, like The Source, The All, or The Absolute. There are also Pagans that do not believe in a Divine entity. Some believe that this entity lives in everything that is organic or made from nature. Some people also believe that this entity lives inside of us too. Many choose not to give the Divine any descriptions or traits. Others believe that the Divine contains both female and male energies. These energies are equal within the Divine; one is not better than the other.

The female energies are similar to our mothers and the women that we know. They can be motherly, caring, nurturing, soft, and loving. The male energies are similar to our fathers and the men that we know. They can be fatherly, protective, strong, and brave. Men and women and boys and girls have both male and female energies inside of them.

Exercise: Think of three female energies that you have and three male. How are these male and female energies different form each other?

The Goddess and the God

Pagans and Wiccans worship the Goddess and the God; there are some that focus more on the Goddess, and there are some Pagans that don't worship either. The **Goddess,** or the Lady, is beautiful, motherly, and wise yet at times she is powerful and dark. The Goddess is represented by the **Moon**. The **God,** or the Lord, is strong, protective, experienced, and a warrior. He is represented by the **Sun**. The Sun's powerful energy gives life to our planet. Plants need sunlight to grow and we need plants to survive. The moonlight at night is also absorbed by the plants. When we eat fruits and vegetables we're also taking in the energy of the Sun and the Moon.

The Sun gives us light and keeps us warm during a cold day. The moonlight lets us see during the dark night as it gently touches our skin. There is a balance between the Sun and the Moon just like there is a balance between the God and the Goddess. The differences between these forces are important in our lives because they help us stay balanced and grounded.

Exercise: Can you think of other things that maintain a balance, like Sun and Moon, day and night, hot and cold, light and dark. What happens when one is stronger than the other?

Deities

Deities is a plural word which means gods and goddesses. The worship of more than one deity is called **polytheism** (poly=many, theos=gods). People that follow polytheistic religions enjoy the liberty of worshiping as many gods as they want. Some polytheistic religions, like Wicca, worship deities from other religions, for example, the Egyptian goddess Isis, the Celtic god Cernunnos, the Greek goddess Aphrodite, or the Anasazi god Manitou. Each deity has certain strengths and characteristics that would make him or her favorable to a specific spell or ritual.

Any deity could be called upon without the formalities of a ritual, for example, if you notice that your garden needs a little help, call on Demeter, Greek goddess of the harvest. You can do this while watering the garden or pulling out weeds; simply say *"Demeter, help my garden become strong and produce many vegetables for my family to eat."* Later in the Fall, after the harvest, make sure you throw any vegetable scraps back into the dirt as a thank you to your garden and Demeter.

Deities are always looking after you. Once you learn more about who they are, you can choose a special god and goddess to hold close to your heart. Sometimes, it is the deities that choose you; like us, they too can feel a strong connection with a human being.

Moon Phases

There is something that is very special about the Moon. Have you ever looked up and saw that the Moon was a full circle or that half of it was missing? The different ways the Moon looks are called **phases**. There are eight lunar phases and they happen because as the Moon is moving around the Earth the sunlight shines on it in different ways.

Sometimes, Pagans and witches get together during a Full Moon or a New Moon to do magick. These Moon meetings or rituals are called **esbats**. Solitaries also perform their own esbats in privacy. The Moon phases help us decide what type of magick to do: Waxing: constructive magick, bringing in things you want. Full: any spell or working that needs extra power. Waning: banishing magick, getting rid of things you don't want. New: magick for new beginnings or a time to rest.

Maiden, Mother, Crone ☽○☾

The Maiden, Mother, and Crone are the three aspects of the Goddess. They represent the three cycles of a woman's life. The Maiden is a young girl, sweet and innocent, learning about life, right and wrong, and romance. The Mother is a mature woman who is nurturing and loving. The Mother can also be strict and become angry and saddened when we disappoint her, but she continues to love us no matter what. The Crone is the old woman, wise and respected. She is a teacher to us.

These three aspects are also represented by the Moon. The growing waxing Moon is the Maiden; the strong full Moon is the Mother; and the dying waning Moon is the Crone. The new Moon is a time for rest for the Goddess as she takes time to replenish her energies and begin a new cycle each month.

The Quarters

Besides the Sun and the Moon, Pagans and Wiccans believe that the compass directions also carry special energies. These directions are East, South, West, and North. They are also called **quarters**. Knowing where the quarters are in relation to where we are standing helps us know what direction we need to go. Think of your house as a big square or a rectangle. Now think of all the windows on each side of your house. Ask your parents to help you determine which direction or quarter each window looks out to.

What about your bedroom window, what direction does it face? If there are windows in your house where you can see the Sun rising in the early morning, that window is facing east because the Sun rises in the east. The opposite side is west, that's where the Sun sets. Once you know the east side of your house, then you can figure out the other directions.

✎ Exercise: Figure out what direction the fences in your yard face. For now just remember these, or if you have enough rocks you can use the rocks to spell the first letter of each direction near each fence.

The Elements

Each quarter has a special **element** and a special color. The elements are Air, Fire, Water, and Earth. The colors are yellow, red, blue, and green. Also in each quarter there is an elemental spirit or guardian who rules and protects over that element's **realm**. Most Pagans believe in a fifth element, Spirit, which is in the center of all the other quarters; its color is purple or white. Spirit is what holds the elements comfortably together like a special glue that is not too sticky or too loose.

Air is the element that gives us life; we breathe air and when we stop breathing we die. We can see why Air is in the East: the day is born with the Sun rising in the East just as we are born with Air filling our baby lungs. Some things that correspond with the Air element are: East, yellow, wind, feathers, incense, smoke, fragrances, smells, wands, wind-chimes, and sounds. Explain why these things represent Air.

The element **Fire** gives us courage and passion; it gives us that little push we sometimes need to be brave. Fire gives us light and warmth. It is the sunlight that plants need to grow and it is the heat needed to cook our food. Some things that correspond with the Fire element are: South, red, candles, dragons, salamanders, lava rocks, swords, athames, electricity, fireplaces, and the Sun. Explain why these things represent Fire.

Water is the element that cleanses our bodies and moves our emotions. Just like a river flows from slow to fast to slow again, our emotions can change from happy to sad, to angry, and to happy again. Did you know that your body is 80% water? Even before you were born, your little baby body was surrounded in fluids inside your mother's belly. Some things that correspond with the Water element are: West, blue, rivers, oceans, lakes, rain, fountains, blood and body fluids, shells, fish, cups, chalices, and the Moon. Explain why these things represent Water.

The element **Earth** gives us stability and protection. This means that Earth gives us a ground to stand on and gives us shelter too. Earth is also the soil and the nutrients that allow plants to grow. Without Earth, plants would not be able to grow deep roots and become strong. Some things that correspond with the Earth element are: North, green, soil, rocks, fossils, bones, trees, seeds, caves, salt, and crystals. Explain why these things represent Earth.

Spirit is the fifth element and is very different from Air, Fire, Water, and Earth. Spirit helps us connect with other people just like it connects the other elements. Spirit is very difficult to describe because it has a different experience for everyone. When we walk on a path of goodness and compassion, our hearts and minds begin to change. This change is called transformation and Spirit makes this happen. Some things that correspond with Sprit are: Center, purple, white, webs, ladders, mazes, empty space, and the universe. Explain why these things represent Sprit.

Exercise: Now that you know what the elements are, if you have some items that represent the elements, place them near the quarter-rocks by the fences in your yard.

Altars and Ritual Tools

Now that you know the basics of deities, the quarters, and the elements, you can start to put an altar together. An **altar** is a surface where your most special representations of deities, spiritual people, and elements are placed for special occasions. An altar could be a table, a window-sill, or anything flat. A special occasion to decorate your altar can be Yule, remembering your ancestors or pets, a birthday, or the first day of spring.

For spring you can place flowers and colorful candles on the altar. You can scatter some seeds which represent the future plants to come. You can also make a little bird nest with twigs and grass and place small stones inside; this represents the baby animals that will be born later in the spring.

Your altar can be anything you want it to be. Some other things to add to your altar are tools. Ritual **tools** are special because they help transmit your energy to where you want it go. Some people keep their tools on their altars while others wrap them in cloth and put them away when not in use. Others choose not to use any tools. Here are some tools that Pagans and witches use:

Athame: a double-edged knife used to direct energy when casting a circle. Not for cutting. Air/East.

Bell/singing bowl: used for calling or invoking deities. Air/East.

Broom/besom: used for sweeping away negative energies but does not physically touch the ground. Water/West.

Salt (in bowl): for cleansing. Earth/North.

Cauldron: an iron pot with three legs. Used for brewing potions and cooking. Water/West.

Chalice: a fancy cup. Water/West.

Incense: for cleansing and sending energies to travel upwards. Air/East.

Pentacle: a five-pointed star inside a circle used for protection. Each point represents the elements. Earth/North.

Candles: a gold candle represents the God and a silver candle represents the Goddess. Colored candles are also placed in each quarter. Fire/South.

Wand: for directing energy. Air/East.

You should cleanse or consecrate your tools as soon as you get them. To **consecrate** means to clean an object with new and positive energy to get rid of any old energy trapped in the object. Once you've consecrated your tools, do not let other people handle them. Your tools are special to you and they hold your energy. When other people touch your tools, their energy can be transmitted and the magick you create may not have the results you intend.

Here is one way to consecrate your tools:

You will need salt (for North/Earth), incense (for East/Air), a white candle (for South/Fire), a small bowl of water (for West/Water), and the tool you will be consecrating; for this example we will use an athame. Ask your parents to help you light the incense and candle.

With the tool in your hands, carefully hold it over the incense and say "Powers of Air cleanse this (tool name) and fill it with my powers for it is mine."

Hold it over the candle flame, carefully, and say "Powers of Fire, cleanse this (tool name) and fill it with my powers for it is mine."

Then sprinkle some water on the tool and say "Powers of Water, cleanse this (tool name) and fill it with my powers for it is mine."

Finally, sprinkle some salt over the tool and say "Powers of Earth, cleanse this (tool name) and fill it with my powers for it is mine."

And now your tool is consecrated, filled with each elemental power and yours, Spirit. Make sure you don't leave the candle burning. You can return the water to the earth in your yard and keep the salt for another ritual.

A simpler way is to cleanse your tools with dirt from your yard. Simply bury them or rub them with dirt. You can also leave your tools in the sunlight and moonlight to cleanse and charge them. There is no wrong way, whatever you do is the right way for you.

A very important tool is the **Book of Shadows**. This is your very own book that is used like a journal and a scrapbook. Here you can write spells, glue articles from magazines, draw, and keep notes in secret alphabets. This is a very magickal book filled with things for only you to see; you can decide if you want to show it to other people. Your first book of shadows doesn't have to be fancy, you can start with a regular notebook and move on to a hardcover book with blank pages.

Spells

We already mentioned that magick is a way to guide or direct energy towards things that we would like to change or things we need a little help with. A **spell** is when we work with magick to reach a specific result. It is very important to always work with magick in a positive way and with good intentions. You always want to consider the well-being of others and never cause harm with your spells. Some of the most popular spells are love spells and money spells but many people have a misunderstanding of these. In a sense, love spells are unethical because you may be forcing someone to fall in love with you. Unethical means that the person is not aware of the spell and did not give permission to have energies manipulated for him. Doing a money spell does not mean that you will become rich overnight. Spells mainly focus on possibilities that are within reach. A spell to help you become more focused at work may lead to a promotion or a raise. While spells can result in receiving money, they are very different from saying "Magick money spell, make me win the lottery and be rich!"

If you want to cast a healing spell because someone close to you is sick, ask them first. The right thing to do is to ask others for permission, some people may not want the help.

Don't expect your spells to give results right away. Spells can be very complicated. It takes time, practice, and patience to be successful with spell casting. Once you know more about magick and learn how to draw in energy, your spells can become more effective. These are lessons to learn as you study the Craft more and more.

You can also write your own spells; they don't have to rhyme. When they contain your own words they are rooted with your inner magickal energy. A spell can be written on a piece of paper and then burned in a cauldron or a fireplace. The spell will travel upwards in the smoke to the sky and beyond. If you live near the beach or a lake you can write your spell on the sand and let the waves take the magick into the ocean.

Spell for finding something:

Visualize the object that is lost. When it is clear in your mind say:

"Magick forces come to be,
What was once lost
Return to me!"

Spell for good grades:

Focus on the test you will be taking and on the material you have been studying. Then say:

"On this test I take today,
I will receive a passing grade.
Earth, Wind, Fire, and Sea,
All good grades, So Mote It Be!"

Exercise: Write a spell, remember to use good intentions. You can bury the piece of paper in your yard and let the earth absorb it.

Casting a Circle

One thing that most Pagans and witches do, especially those in covens or open circles, is to cast a circle for rituals and magick-work. Some cast simpler circles and others don't cast circles at all. Those that cast circles do it mainly for maintaining the traditions of long ago and because it feels right to them. A circle protects the group or the solitary from negative energies coming inside. It acts like a big dome that holds all the magick and energies within, like a big bubble.

Once the circle is cast, the rule is that no one should leave or enter because it can create a doorway for negative energies to enter. This is why it is important to always be on time; some places lock the main door so that those who are late do not come in and disrupt the ritual and the circle. Just in case, someone is assigned as a door or gate-keeper; this person makes sure that he opens and closes an energetic door when others need to enter or leave the circle. There are many ways to cast a circle and as you continue your studies you will learn the different ways that each tradition does it.

Here is one simple way to cast a circle: Decide where you will cast your circle. Make sure it is an open space without furniture and wide enough to hold two of you with your arms stretched out at your sides. If you have tools, gather them: broom, bowl with water and salt, incense or a feather, athame or wand or your finger, quarter candles or items colored for each quarter, God and Goddess candles, or items colored gold and silver, **cakes and ale** (a simple snack like cookies and juice), a small plate and cup or chalice.

First, place the quarter candles or items at each quarter. If you're using candles, make sure they are placed on something sturdy. For safety reasons, you don't have to light the candles, you can visualize that they will be lit. You can also use the battery operated candles and decorate them as you'd like. Place a small altar in the center of the circle. The God and Goddess candles can be placed here along with the cakes and ale and any other special items you would like.

Now it's time to cleanse the space. Traditionally this is done by walking three times, clockwise or **deosil** (sunwise), starting at the East quarter or North depending on the tradition.

For the first walk, grab the broom and sweep the perimeter of the circle, remember that the broom does not touch the ground. If you don't have a broom you can use your hands and arms in a swaying motion.

For the second walk, sprinkle salt water (just a little bit) around the circle; this is like giving the area a bath. For the third walk, grab the incense or a feather and walk around the circle. The space is now clean.

To cast the circle, grab the athame or wand or you can use your pointed index finger. Stand near the center of the circle and point low towards the East quarter. Use your imagination and see the light coming out of your wand or finger. Turn around clockwise as you draw a full circle. The circle is cast now.

Now it's time to invite the elementals. If you are allowed to light candles this is when you will light them as you are speaking to each quarter. Otherwise you can hold the colored item and place it down, or visualize that the candle is lit. Starting at the East, say "Powers of the East, element of Air, I invite you to my circle, please protect me." Then move to the South quarter and say "Powers of the South, element of Fire, I invite you to my circle, please protect me." Do the same for West and North. Now the elementals are present.

Next invite the God and Goddess. Some traditions invite the God first so he can protect the path for the Goddess. Other traditions only invite the Goddess. Stand in front of the God candle or item and say "Powerful Lord, Father of all, I invite you to my circle, please protect me." And for the Goddess say "Beautiful Lady, Mother of all, I invite you to my circle, please protect me." The God and Goddess are now inside.

Now you can do anything you'd like in the circle. You can do spells, read, draw, or whatever feels right for you. Remember not to leave the circle. You can also enjoy your cakes and ale. First break a piece of your snack and place it on the small plate. Then pour some of the juice in the cup or chalice. This is an offering for the God and Goddess as a thank you for being in your circle this day.

Once you're done, it is time to dismiss the powers. Traditionally, this is done in reverse and counter-clockwise or **widdershins**. First dismiss the Goddess, say "Thank you Lady for being in my circle, I bid you farewell." Do the same for the God. Then dismiss the elementals starting with North, walking counter-clockwise, say "Thank you Powers of Earth for being in my circle, I bid you farewell." Do the same for the West, South, and East. Finally, it is time to open the circle. With your finger or tool, pointing at the East, move around counter-clockwise, imagining the light being absorbed back into you.

Once complete, you can send that light towards the sky and towards the ground and say "As above, so below." Some traditions end the circle by chanting "The circle is open, but never broken, May the God and the Goddess be forever in your heart. Merry meet, and merry part, and merry meet again."

Remember, your circle does not need to include all of those details. If you feel comfortable visualizing a circle without doing all the walking and the motions, that is fine. Or you don't have to cast a circle at all. Do what feels right for you. This way is just to teach you what some Pagans and Wiccans do.

Herb Garden

Herbs are plants that we use for cooking and for medicine. They have natural magickal properties that help us with spells. Herbs are so special that sometimes we can just hold a small branch or a leaf of the herb in our hand or just smell it and we immediately feel a sense of happiness and calmness. Consider growing your own herb garden with herbs that you like, perhaps mint, lavender, sage, rosemary, basil, and lemon verbena. If your herb garden is outside, make sure you water it often because the strong sunlight can evaporate the water from the dirt.

A garden outside can be a home for dragonflies, ladybugs, and honey bees. If your herb garden is inside, make sure that it is by a window so that it can receive the Sun's rays. Also, make sure that the herbs are in pots or in containers that drain well so that the roots don't rot. An indoor herb garden will add a special scent to the room. Some herbs are dangerous or toxic so make sure you have herbs that are safe, especially if you have a younger brother or sister.

Drum Circles

One way for a group to raise energy is to play instruments, but even more energy can be raised in a drum circle. Drum circles are exactly that, drum players arranged in a circle. The players usually play different types of drums and other hand instruments. Drum circles can take place before, during, and after rituals. They can also be a reason for people to gather, talk, play music, and dance.

When the weather is warm or cool, drum circles usually take place outside with a bonfire in the center. Being outdoors connects us with nature as we dance to the drum beat. When it's too cold outside, drum circles take place indoors, in buildings, basements, or living rooms. Music and drum beats can have a strong effect in people's brains. The rhythmic beats create a meditative state for some people; they become the beat. For some, this beat connects them with the spirits.

Exercise: If you have a drum, make up some beats. You can start with three to six beats and repeat them over and over. Change the rhythm from time to time, slow, fast, slow. Drum soft, drum hard.

Chants

Chants are songs or vocalizations used to raise energy for magick-work or just to sing for fun. Chants can also be considered as prayers that are sung to the gods and the goddesses. There are many, many books and websites that contain traditional and modern chants. Chants are used during rituals, drum circles, or just at home. Like spells, chants are special because they hold unique energies for specific results. If you wanted to call the elements you can sing the popular chant Air I Am: "Air I am, Fire I am, Water, Earth and Spirit I am!" Chants are more powerful if you make them up yourself. This way you are using your own energy and the results can be greater. Traditional chants are short and also rhyme. If you have a hard time thinking of lines that rhyme, don't worry about it; just chant what comes from your heart.

Exercise: Write a chant about your favorite element. Keep it short, about four lines. Take your drum and give your chant a beat!

Here are some popular chants:

The Earth is our Mother

The Earth is our mother,
We must take care of her,
The Earth is our mother,
We must take care of her.
Hey yana ho yana,
Hey yan yan,
Hey yana, ho yana,
Hey yan yan.

We Are a Circle

We are a circle,
Within a circle,
With no beginning
And never ending.

We All Come from the Goddess

We all come from the Goddess,
And to her we shall return,
Like a drop of rain
Flowing to the ocean.

Spirits of Fire

Spirit of fire come to us,
We will kindle the fire,
Spirit of fire come to us,
We will kindle the fire.
We will kindle the fire,
Dance the magic circle
round,
We will kindle the fire,
We will kindle the fire.

Seasons

Throughout the year we see changes in the plants and trees around us, and feel the changing of the weather on our skin. These changes are called the **seasons**. Our planet goes through a cycle of four seasons each year as a result of its orbit around the Sun. The seasons are Spring, Summer, Autumn or Fall, and Winter and they tell the story of the beautiful changes that Nature goes through every year. Some people live each year according to the seasons because they have a deep connection with Nature.

After the snow melts and the sunlight is stronger, Spring brings the rebirth of plants and animals. The warmth calls animals out of their burrows and caves. The Sun's energy penetrates through the soil and brings forth sprouts of crocuses, future flowers, herbs, trees, and crops. At home we are preparing our gardens and are planting the tiny seeds that will hopefully bring a bountiful harvest.

Summer is warmer, sometimes hot. The animals are out chasing insects; the babies from late Spring are now discovering things on their own. Our gardens are growing; some plants are showing the tiny buds that will turn into vegetables. People gather outside and enjoy the shade from the trees and the warm nights.

The weather starts to cool in Autumn. Our little animal friends are busy collecting food in their burrows in preparation for Winter. The garden is ready for harvesting, maybe its second or third harvest of the season by now. The trees are dropping their leaves while some yellow ones are still hanging on. Like the animals, we bring our crops inside and prepare them for storage.

The cold Winter has arrived and possibly the first of many snowflakes. The animals are hard to find now, some are sleeping underground, and some leave little foot trails on the snow. The snow covers the ground, our gardens, and our roofs. We sit inside around the fireplace and are thankful for having shelter and warmth. This is a time to think of all the things we did throughout the year and come up with new goals for the year to come. Soon the snow will melt and we can start our new goals and promises along with a fresh, new garden, and our furry friends.

Exercise: Set up a small altar outside. Decorate it with items that represent the current season. Leave some safe treats for the animals to enjoy, like bread and nuts. Change your outside altar each season.

8 Sabbats: The Wheel of the Year

Wiccans and most Pagans celebrate eight **sabbats** or festivals throughout the year. The sabbats are divided into Fire festivals (or cross-quarter festivals) and Solar festivals (or quarter festivals or lesser sabbats). The Fire festivals are associated with the element Fire while the Solar festivals relate to the equinoxes and solstices (the seasons). The progression of each sabbat around the calendar is called "turning the **wheel of the year**." Why a wheel? When the sabbats are written on a circle with eight equal parts, the lines dividing the sabbats look like the spokes of a wheel, like a wagon wheel.

Some people celebrate all eight sabbats, others just celebrate the Fire festivals, and others only celebrate the Solar festivals. Covens and circles gather for ritual and celebration during the sabbats while the solitaries practice at home. The wheel of the year was the way our ancestors lived and connected with Nature. The wheel also tells the story of the God and the Goddess, their birth and death, and their love for each other.

Samhain (Oct 31 Northern Hemisphere; May 1 Southern Hemisphere; Fire/Cross quarter festival): Samhain (pronounced sah-wain or sah-ween) marks the death aspect of the cycle but is also considered the New Year for Wiccans. Depending on where you live, Samhain may be considered the third harvest of the season if the first frost has not yet set in. At Samhain we see empty fields, the harvests have come and go, and very little green is showing. This is the death of the Sun God as he has been growing weak since Litha. It is also the time when the Goddess is the Crone, old and wise. She will miss her lover the Sun God but she continues to carry their child who will be born again in Yule, as he does every year. Samhain is a festival that celebrates darkness and death. It welcomes the idea that death is part of our circle of life, everything that lives must die. This is also a time to remember our ancestors and call out to spirits from the past. The veil between the living world and the spirit world is thin on this night; use it wisely to connect with your ancestors.

Yule (Dec 21/22 NH; June 21/22 SH; Solar/Quarter festival): Yule, or the Winter Solstice, is the shortest day of the year and the longest night. Even though it is cold and dark outside, this festival celebrates the birth of the Sun God and light. After the shortest day passes, the days that follow will become longer and longer and the Sun God will grow stronger.

People gather in their homes to celebrate. They bring in pine trees, ivy, and holly to remember that the world outside will soon turn green again; they light candles and decorate their homes with lights to bring in the sunlight back into their hearts; they feast on many types of foods to show that they are surviving the cold winter. The plants and animals are still sleeping underneath the snow; this is also a time to think of goals deep in your mind and of projects to start for the year to come.

Imbolc (Feb 1/2 NH; Aug 1/2 SH; Fire/Cross quarter festival): We can see and feel that winter is loosening its grip on our surroundings. The first of flowers and plants push upwards from the wet ground. Imbolc is a reminder that Spring is on its way. It is also a festival that honors the Celtic fire goddess Brighid (pronounced breed). Brighid is the protector of women, children, animals, and Spring. She clears the snow and brings the warmth so that life can emerge once again. It is customary to light candles during Imbolc to help the Sun God continue to gather his strength while Brighid uses her motherly qualities to help him.

Ostara (March 21/22 NH; Sept 21/22 SH; Solar/Quarter festival): Ostara, or the Spring Equinox, is one of the two days when day and night are of equal length. It also means that Spring is finally here! We celebrate the Germanic goddess Eostre as a fertility deity and the upcoming abundance of life. Hares and eggs are also fertility symbols and are popular during this festival.

The Easter Bunny and Easter eggs originated in pagan times while celebrating Ostara. Today, pagan children continue to decorate eggs to hide and find in their yards. The Sun God is now growing and has found the young maiden aspect of the Goddess. They are playful with each other and frolic about in the fields. During the equinox, many Pagans meet in sacred places to celebrate.

Beltane (May 1 NH; Oct 31 SH; Fire/Cross quarter festival): Beltane is May Day, a festival that celebrates fertility and love. The God and the Goddess are young adults; they fall in love, and come together. They become the Green Man and the May Queen. Their union is celebrated by dancing around the May Pole and jumping over bale fires. Jumping over bale fires was a tradition of long ago that was thought to bring luck and abundance for the harvests to come, both in cattle and crops. Everything is green on Beltane. The Sun is out and romance is in the air.

Litha (June 21/22 NH; Dec 21/22 SH; Solar/Quarter festival): Litha is the Summer Solstice, also called Midsummer. This is the longest day of the year and the first day of Summer. The Sun God is the strongest on this day. His powers and radiance are felt throughout the lands. Pagans and Wiccans gather in drum circles to celebrate the Sun because when this day is over, the days become shorter and the Sun becomes weak. The Goddess is carrying the Sun Child in her belly. Both she and the Sun God know that once the Sun God dies, the Sun Child will be born and become the new Sun God. Wiccans know this too and they celebrate this day to hold on to the Sun God as long as they can.

Lughnasadh (Aug 1/2 NH; Feb 1/2 SH; Fire/Cross quarter festival): Lughnasadh, or Llamas, is the first harvest. It celebrates the Celtic God Lugh, a fire deity, the provider of sunlight and energy to the crops that are about to be harvested. This is the harvest of grains and cereal. Lughnasadh is also a time for people to continue to care for their gardens and farms; long ago for our ancestors these harvests were important because they determined the probability of survival.

Mabon (Sept 21/22 NH; March 21/22 SH; Solar/Quarter festival): Mabon, or Modron, is the Autumnal or Fall Equinox. Day and night are equal again, but the days will get shorter and the nights longer. Mabon is the second harvest. It is a time to give thanks to what the Earth and the Sun have provided us. We prepare ourselves with bringing our crops inside; we buy warmer clothes, and start to leave the summer days behind us. On this day of balance, we focus on the things we still need to work on so we may find balance in our lives and within ourselves. The Sun God is starting his journey to the Underworld which ends in Samhain; the Goddess also begins her final transformation; yet the promise of the Sun Child lies ahead in Yule.

Numerology 1 2 3 4 5 6 7 8 9

Numerology is the study of how numbers influence our lives. Just like the zodiac signs describe certain characteristics and personalities, numbers do the same. There are several numerology categories and here we'll look at two of them: your birthdate numerology and your name numerology. It's interesting to see what these two numbers are because both of these categories are very different. Your birthdate is unchangeable but your name can take different forms.

Finding out your birthdate number (also called the Life Path Number) is easy. Simply add all the numbers in your birthdate until you end up with one digit. For example, if someone's birthdate is November 16, 1998 or 11/16/1998, add: 26/02/2003 = 2+6+2+2+3 = 15 = 1+5 = 6

1 + 1 + 1 + 6 + 1 + 9 + 9 + 8 = 36 = 3 + 6 = 9

The birthdate number is 9.

For your name number (also called the Personality Number), you can choose to use your full name at birth or use your nickname or a form of your name that you connect with. Each letter in your name corresponds to a number, then add them up just like you did with your birthdate. Look at the letters and number chart to determine your name number.

A	B	C	D	E	F	G	H	I
1	2	3	4	5	6	7	8	9
J	K	L	M	N	O	P	Q	R
1	2	3	4	5	6	7	8	9
S	T	U	V	W	X	Y	Z	
1	2	3	4	5	6	7	8	

Daniel Thomas Shan

Mehgan Beckett Brooks

= 77 = 7 + 7 = 14 = 1 + 4 = 5

Once you have your birthdate and name numbers, find your number below and read what it says about you.

1 leader, independent, ambitious, confident

2 gentle, sensitive, caring, peaceful

3 joyful, optimistic, sociable, expressive

4 worker, stable, structure, reliable

5 freedom and fun-loving, diverse, adventurous

6 family, love, home, harmony

7 intuition, quiet, spiritual, life

8 manager, business-oriented, organized,

9 teacher, wisdom, giver, experienced

Alphabets

Alphabets help us learn a language different from ours. Some alphabets have different letters or symbols and sounds. Some of them have more or less letters than the 26 in our ABC's. Some alphabets are more than just letters where each symbol stands for something, like the Ogham Tree alphabet or the Elder Futhark used for **divination**. Other alphabets, like the Theban, were developed and then used as a secret way to communicate. Here are some alphabets that you can have fun with and write your own secret messages.

Theban Alphabet

Ogham Tree Alphabet (Letter/Tree)

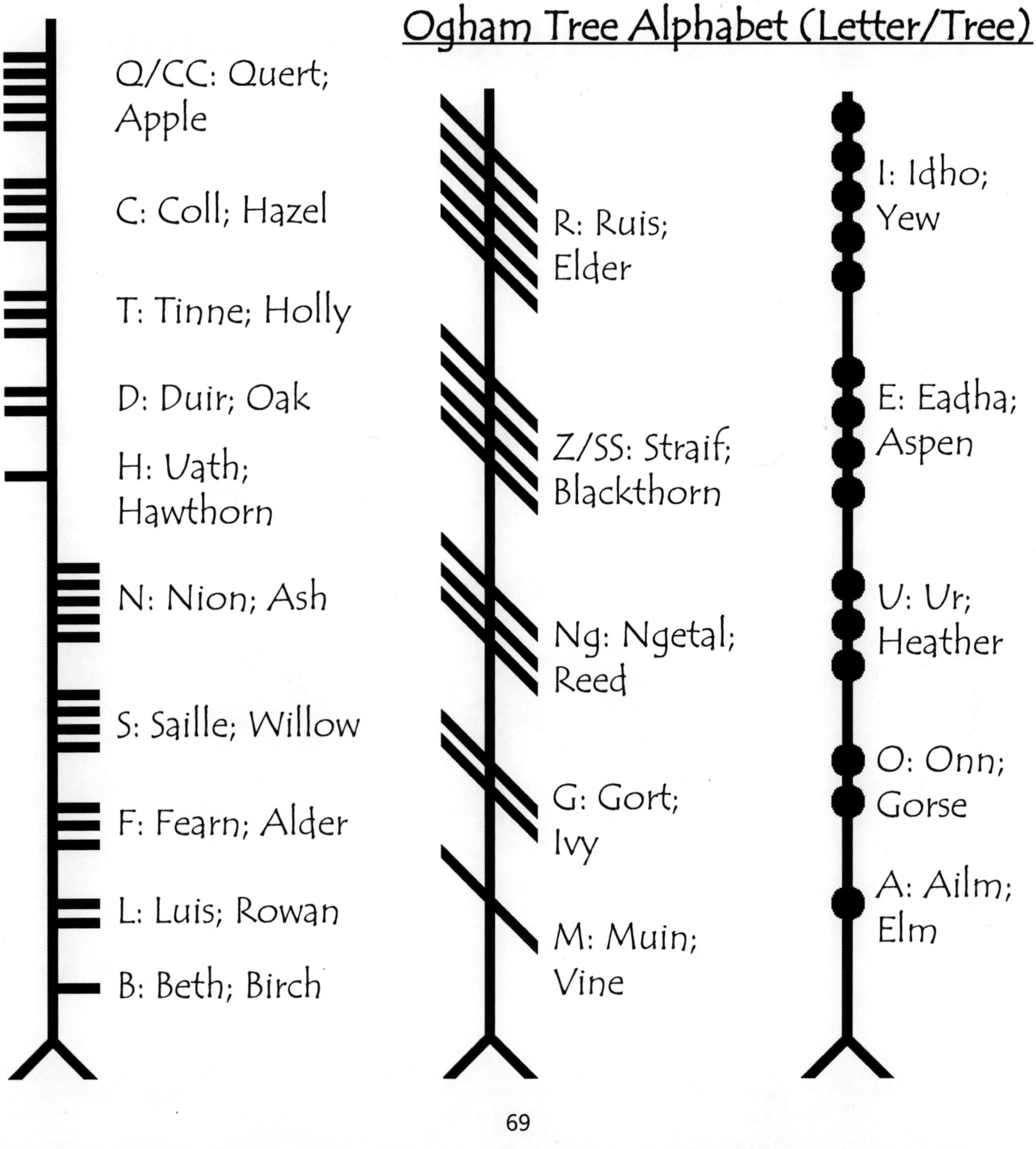

ELDER FUTHARK RUNE ALPHABET

ᚠ F: Fehu	ᚺ H: Hagalaz	ᛏ T: Teiwaz
ᚢ U: Uruz	ᚾ N: Nauthiz	ᛒ B: Berkana
ᚦ Th: Thurisaz	ᛁ I: Isa	ᛖ E: Ehwaz
ᚨ A: Ansuz	ᛃ J/Y: Jera	ᛗ M: Mannaz
ᚱ R: Raido	ᛇ E: Eihwaz	ᛚ L: Laguz
ᚲ K: Kenaz	ᛈ P: Perthro	ᛜ Ng: Ingus
ᚷ G: Gebo	ᛉ Z: Algiz	ᛟ O: Othila
ᚹ W/V: Wunjo	ᛊ S: Sowulo	ᛞ D: Dagaz

Planets

Did you know that the word *planet* comes from an ancient Greek word that means *to wander*? **Astronomers** from ancient times studied the night sky and noticed that some stars would stay still and other stars would wander across the sky from night to night and month to month. They called these wandering stars *planets* and named them after Roman deities: Mercury, Venus, Earth*, Mars, Jupiter, Saturn, Uranus, Neptune, and Pluto. Our planet Earth is the only one not named after a Roman god. Look at the chart to learn more about each planet.

☿ Mercury: Messenger of the Gods

♀ Venus: Goddess of love/beauty

⊕ Earth: Our home

♂ Mars: God of war

♃ Jupiter: King of the gods

♄ Saturn: God of time

⛢ Uranus: Father of Saturn

♆ Neptune: God of the seas

♇ Pluto: God of death

Zodiac Signs

Another word derived from ancient times is *zodiac*, it means *circle*, *belt*, or *circle of animals*. The ancient zodiac only included animals but this has changed as it now includes animals, objects, and humans. In Western Astrology there are twelve zodiac signs which determine certain characteristics we possess at the month and day we are born. These signs are: Aquarius, Pisces, Aries, Taurus, Gemini, Cancer, Leo, Virgo, Libra, Scorpio, Sagittarius, and Capricorn. Some **astrologers** argue that there is a thirteenth sign called Ophiuchus. Each sign is masculine or feminine, positive or negative, and passive or active. Again, we see the importance of balance in our lives. There are other zodiacs that people around the world use like the Chinese and Vedic zodiacs. Western astrology considers the position of the Sun, the Moon, and the planets at the moment we are born; this gives us unique personalities even when we share the same sign.

♒ Aquarius (Jan 20 – Feb 18), The Water-Bearer, Planet Uranus, Element Air, Masculine, Fixed. Distant, eccentric, independent.

♓ Pisces (Feb 19 – Mar 20), The Fish, Planet Neptune, Element Water, Feminine, Mutable. Ambitious, mysterious, impressionable.

♈ Aries (Mar 21 – Apr 19), The Ram, Planet Mars, Element Fire, Masculine, Cardinal. Assertive, forthright, urgent.

♉ Taurus (Apr 20 – May 20), The Bull, Planet Venus, Element Earth, Feminine, Fixed. Possessive, permanent, reliable.

♊ <u>Gemini</u> (May 21- Jun 20), The Twins, Planet Mercury, Element Air, Masculine, Mutable. Adaptable, communicative, versatile.

♋ <u>Cancer</u> (Jun 21 – Jul 22), The Crab, Moon, Element Water, Feminine, Cardinal. Protective, sensitive, loving.

♌ <u>Leo</u> (Jul 23 – Aug 22), The Lion, Sun, Element Fire, Masculine, Fixed. Creative, powerful, self-centered.

♍ <u>Virgo</u> (Aug 23 – Sep 22), The Virgin, Planet Mercury, Element Earth, Feminine, Mutable. Analytical, hardworking, giver.

♎ <u>Libra</u> (Sep 23 – Oct 22), The Scales, Planet Venus, Element Air, Masculine, Cardinal. Balanced, sympathetic, charming.

♏ <u>Scorpio</u> (Oct 23 – Nov 21), The Scorpion, Planet Pluto, Element Water, Feminine, Fixed. Intense, passionate, magnetic.

♐ <u>Sagittarius</u> (Nov 22 – Dec 21), The Archer, Planet Jupiter, Element Fire, Masculine, Mutable. Philosophical, searching, playful.

♑ <u>Capricorn</u> (Dec 22 – Jan 19), The Goat, Planet Saturn, Element Earth, Feminine, Cardinal. Ambitious, patient, structure.

Choosing a Magickal Name

Now that you have learned some of the basics of Wicca, you can start thinking of a magickal name. This name is also called a Pagan name, Wiccan name, or Circle name. Most people with a magickal name keep their name secret and only share it with others in their circle. There are several ways to choose a magickal name. One way is to mix and match the names of things you feel a connection with. For example, if your favorite color is silver and your favorite bird is an owl, then your name can be Silver Owl. You can add a third name if you want, like Ivy Silver Owl.

Another way to choose a name is by using numerology. Some people prefer their magickal name number to match their birthdate number. This can take some time because it can be difficult to make the numbers match, but you can change the spelling of the name so the numbers match. This could be a very unique magickal name that nobody else will have.

A Year-and-a-Day

The timeframe of a **year-and-a-day** is a tradition for witches of long ago. For new witches or **seekers** of the Nature path, a year-and-a-day is a time of study and a time to experience the wonderful things the Craft has to offer. During this time you will focus on the seasons and the Wheel of the Year. As Nature is going through changes outside, we pay attention to how our lives are changing too. This is a time to learn how Nature affects us and how we connect with it.

There are books that take the seeker or student through lessons and activities for a year-and-a-day. You can also have a teacher to guide you. Once the student has completed this period, he can do an initiation ceremony by himself (solitary), by his teacher, or with others he trusts (a circle). The next chapter talks about dedication and initiation ceremonies. Also, a year-and-a-day doesn't have to be 366 days exactly; everyone has a different path, some people may move quicker and some people may take longer. All that matters is that you feel ready to move on to the next part of your path, whatever that may be.

Self-Dedication for the Solitary

After reading this book you will have an understanding of what the Pagan and Wiccan paths are about. If you are ready to continue to learn more perhaps you'd like to do a dedication ceremony. A dedication ceremony means that you will dedicate your time to continue to learn about Paganism and/or Wicca and how to become one with Nature. A dedication usually takes place before starting the year-and-a-day period. A person who dedicates himself to this path is called a **dedicant**.

Here is a simple ritual for a self-dedication ceremony. Gather items that represent the elements. Place these items in their corresponding quarters. You can either be in the center of these items or they can be in front of you so you can see them all. Cast a circle if you choose to. Imagine that you are surrounded by a beautiful light that is protecting you. Look at your element items and think of a way that each element can help you in your future studies in the path. Ask the elements to protect you and guide you throughout your lessons. You can finish the ritual by saying "I am dedicating myself to a path of goodness, of being kind to others, my loved ones and **familiars**, and caring for plants and nature. I will continue to study Nature as long as my heart is fully in it, and I will not use magick to harm other beings in any way. So mote it be!" Open the circle, put the items away, and enjoy the many things you will learn! You can write about your dedication, the date, and your experience in your Book of Shadows.

Initiation Into the Path

For those that continue and complete the year-and-a-day, an initiation ceremony is the traditional thing to do. The initiation ceremony is more complex than a dedication ceremony because it includes many of the things learned during the year-and-a-day. Those that are solitary perform a self-initiation ceremony and those who participate with a circle have an initiation ceremony led by the high priest and high priestess of that group. Once a person is initiated, he or she can be called an **initiate** and possibly a priest or priestess.

Continuing the Path

As you continue the path you will learn many lessons from both Pagan and Wiccan traditions, like divination, candle and color magick, meditation and visualization, and invoking the spirits and ancestors. You will learn about Rites of Passage like Wiccaning, Moon-rites, and Handfasting. Other lessons include the Thirteen Goals of a Witch, the Wiccan Rede, and the Witch's Rune. These last three are Wiccan guidelines of how one on this path must behave and have the proper intentions when working magick. The most important lesson is the Rule or the Law of Three. **The Rule of Three** means that however you behave, those energies will come back to you times three, or three times as powerful. For example, if you intentionally took something that was not yours, it is likely that you will be punished in return; perhaps a thief breaks into your house and steals things from your room. The Rule of Three also works when doing good deeds. If you notice that a person walking drops a $10 bill and you let him know, who knows, maybe he'll say thank you and let you keep the money.

But there is one rule that is more important than any other rule...An It Harm None, Do What Ye Will. This is the last line in the Wiccan Rede. It means that as long as it doesn't harm anyone or anything, then go ahead and do what you'd like. This is the number one rule for Wiccans and Pagans. These Nature paths are about showing compassion and love to all that lives on the planet. If we love each other, and love plants and animals, why would we want to harm them purposely?

As you continue on your path many questions may come to mind. With time, you will feel a stronger connection with Nature and will be able to answer some of these questions. Sometimes there are questions that we may never have the answer to, so focus on what is important now and try not to worry about the things that can't be changed. The spirits, our ancestors, and Nature are always looking after us. Welcome them with perfect love and perfect trust!

So mote it be!

Glossary

Adept- a person who is very knowledgeable and proficient in the Craft. Usually the last stage of study: seeker, dedicant, initiate, adept.

Agnosticism- the view that the existence or the nonexistence of a God or Divine entity can be known. An agnostic is a person who doubts or questions the existence of a God.

Air- the element corresponding with the East quarter. Some characteristics of Air are: yellow, communication, wind, and sounds.

Altar- a flat surface decorated with ritual tools, sabbats representations, or any items used as a center piece for ritual, spells, or celebrations.

Astrology- the study of the position and aspects of planets, stars, and other celestial bodies and how they influence human life and events on Earth. A person who studies astrology is an astrologer.

Astronomy- the study of the universe, planets, stars, and other forms of matter and energy beyond planet Earth. A person who studies astronomy is an astronomer.

Atheism- the view that God or a Divine being does not exist. An atheist is a person who does not believe in God.

Book of Shadows- a secret journal where a witch keeps personal details, spells, and rituals.

Cakes and ale- a food and drink consumed and shared while in a ritual circle after it is offered to the God and Goddess as a gratitude for their attendance in the circle. Also known as an offering or libation.

Chants- songs or vocalizations used to raise energy for magick-work

Circle- (1) A community of people with similar Pagan beliefs that perform rituals and magick together. An **open circle** is a community that welcomes all traditions and all peoples. (2) A sacred space that contains energies to perform magick or spells; casting a circle.

Consecrate- to cleanse an item and infuse it with one's own positive and personal energy.

Coven- a traditional group of witches, sometimes 13, who may be strict about membership guidelines.

Dedicant- a person who is simply starting the Wiccan path and is not yet initiated. One of the stages of study: seeker, dedicant, initiate, adept.

Deity- a god or goddess; plural: deities.

Deosil- to move in a clockwise or sunwise direction. Used in certain traditions to cast circles and invoke spirits.

Divination- the act of foretelling future events by using divination tools like Tarot cards, runes, and scrying mirrors.

Divine- something or someone that is superhuman characterized as goodness and heavenly.

Drum circle- a tradition in Pagan cultures where drums and other instruments are played during rituals and celebrations.

Earth- the element corresponding with the North quarter. Some characteristics of Earth are: green, protection, ground, and plants.

East- one of the four quarters or directions; corresponds with Air.

Elements- the substances of which the universe is composed; Air, Fire, Water, Earth, and Spirit.

Esbat- Moon-phase gatherings or lunar celebrations to work magick, spells, and celebrate deities.

Fire- the element corresponding with the South quarter. Some characteristics of Fire are: red, passion, heat, and courage.

Familiars- an animal, sometimes a pet, with whom one feels a strong connection with spiritually; a totem animal.

Gaia- in Greek mythology she is the goddess of the Earth. Gaia is honored as Mother Earth, the one who life sprouted from.

God- the male aspect or personification of the Divine or Supreme Being. In Paganism, the Sun represents the God.

Goddess- the female aspect or personification of the Divine or Supreme Being. In Paganism, the Moon represents the Goddess.

Herbs- special plants which hold medicinal and healing properties and are also used for cooking, ambience, and spells.

Initiate- a person who completes the dedicant stage usually after a year-and-a-day and is initiated. One of the stages of study: seeker, dedicant, initiate, adept.

Magick- the way that energies are manipulated to achieve a specific result or goal.

Monotheism- the view that only one God or Supreme Being exists and there is no place for other deities.

Moon- in Paganism, the Moon is the celestial body which represents the Goddess and all female energies. Some characteristics are: wisdom, mother, and guide.

Mythology- traditional stories or myths relating to deities of ancient cultures which gave an explanation of people's surroundings to make sense of the world.

Nature- our surroundings which include plants, animals, weather, the seasons, the elements, and the planet's natural state.

Nature religions- religions which main focus is the homeostasis or well-being of our planet.

North- one of the four quarters or directions; corresponds with Earth.

Numerology- the study of numbers and their influence on human life.

Organized religions- mainly the religions of Christianity, Judaism, and Islam which abide by a specific book of scriptures and a set belief system.

Paganism- a category of religion outside of the organized religions. Some Pagan religions include ancient Roman, Greek, and Egyptian religions, Wicca, and Indigenous religions.

Phases- the different views of the Moon we see during its 28 day cycle. Each Moon phase holds and releases unique energies desired for magick-work.

Polytheism- the view of the existence of more than one god.

Quarters- the directions of how we move through space: East, South, West, and North. Each quarter corresponds to an element and carries unique magickal properties.

Realm- a place or world separate from the world we experience every day; the spirit realm, the elemental realms, the living realm.

Religion- a belief system mainly of ethical behaviors which leads to a path to a deeper connection with a Supreme Being, no Supreme Being, or the individual's surroundings.

Ritual- a gathering within a circle or individually to perform magick or celebrate esbats or sabbats.

Rule of Three- a principle that holds that all actions come back more powerful, whether positive or negative. Also known as the Law of Three or the Law of Return.

Sabbats- the eight holidays or festivals celebrated by Wiccans based on pagan traditions, broken down into Fire festivals and Solar festivals.

Seasons- the changes in climate that the planet goes through as a result of its orbit around the Sun. The four seasons are: Spring, Summer, Autumn, Winter.

Seeker- a person who seeks knowledge in specific matters. In Wicca, a seeker is someone who is new to Wicca and explores this path to see how it suits his life. One of the stages of study: seeker, dedicant, initiate, adept.

Solitary- a person or practitioner who practices religion in private.

South- one of the four quarters or directions; corresponds with Fire.

Spirit- the element corresponding with the center of a circle. Some characteristics of Spirit are: purple, transformation, meditation, and connection.

Sun- in Paganism, the Sun is the celestial body which represents the God and all masculine energies. Some characteristics are: strength, power, and father.

Tools- items used for directing energy and for magick-work mostly during rituals and spells.

Water- the element corresponding with the West quarter. Some characteristics of Water are: blue, intuition, dreams, and motion.

West- one of the four quarters or directions; corresponds with Water.

Wheel of the year- the progression of the sabbats and the interconnectedness between Nature and human life.

Wicca- a religion with beliefs, practices, and traditions of ancient times honoring a Divine concept, god(s), and goddess(es) or any combination of these. Wiccans mainly revere nature and its cycles as the guidelines of daily activity year after year.

Widdershins- to move in a counter-clockwise direction. Used in certain traditions to banish spirits and open circles.

Witch- a Wiccan, Pagan, or a person of any religion who uses magick by manipulating energies or relies on Nature to determine the outcomes.

World religions- see *Organized religions*.

Year-and-a-day- a timeframe of studying the Wiccan path before becoming initiated; usually starts with the dedicant stage.

Acknowledgements

Photography credits: **1stPage**: Aldborough May Day 2010 - Dancing Around the Maypole by Steenbergs, flickr Creative Commons; **Foreword:** Kiftsgate Court Gardens- Statue of Mother and Child by Elliott Brown, flickr Creative Commons; **HowToUseThisBook**: A Child's Garden of Verses, flickr Creative Commons Public Domain; **Collage:** Lonely Prayers by Howie Le, flickr Creative Commons; **WhatIsReligion:** A Day at Kindergarden by amrufm, flickr Creative Commons; Laos Luang Prabang84 by mckaysavage, flickr Creative Commons; Aum, Christian Cross, Yin Yang, Ahimsa, Black Star of David from Wikimedia Commons; Dharmacakra, Bahai Star, Islam Symbol, Simple Labarum, Pentacle from Wikimedia Commons; African Children's Choir by Rob Swystun, flickr Creative Commons; 20120607-DSC07992 by Clemens V Vogelsang(vauvau), flicker Creative Commons; **WhatIsPaganism:** Culture by Jordan Wade (greyshine), flickr Creative Commons; Petroglyphs on Atlatl Rock by Michael Bentley, flickr Creative Commons; It's a Bunch of Rocks by Phelyan Sanjoin (hpeguk), flickr Creative Commons; The Green Goddess by Jayel Aheram, flickr Creative Commons; Gathered by Steve Jurvetson, flickr Creative Commons; Puddles in Luss by Joccay, flickr Creative Commons; **WhatIsWicca:** The Witch's Craic by Barry Lewis (Sir Hectimere), flick Creative Commons; **TypesOfWicca:** Nanaimo Pagan Pride Day by Kam Abott (Kam's World), flickr Creative Commons; Belle Nell by Hermetic Hermit, flickr Creative Commons; **MagickAndWitches:** Hecate by Cornelia Kopp (AlicePopkorn), flickr Creative Commons; Umbanda by Aline Scaravelli, flickr Creative Commons; **TheDivine:** Stars Over Ocotillo Wells by John Lemieux, flickr Creative Commons; **GoddessAndGod:** DSC_3068 by Peter Dyakov, flickr Creative Commons; Sun or Compass by Anne-Lisse Heinrichs (snigl3t), flickr Creative Commons; Near Full Moon Tonight by PsJeremy; Moon 290 by Rocky Raybell, flickr Creative Commons; **Deities:** Venus_figure,_Laussel,_replica by HTO, Wikimedia Commons; Dancing Mother Goddess Varahi by Wonderlane, flickr Creative Commons; IMG 8144 by Brian Norwood, flickr Creative Commons; Pan by Liz West (Muffet), flickr Creative Commons; **MoonPhases:** All eight photographs: Full Moon, Waxing Gibbous, First Quarter, Waxing Crescent, New Moon, Waning Crescent, Third Quarter, Waning Gibbous by Nasa Goddard Photo and Video, flickr Creative Commons; **MaidenMotherCrone:** Three Graces by Rojer, flickr Creative Commons; Female Figurines by Tilemahos Efthimiadis, flickr Creative Commons; Ecuador Moon Phases by glorious journey photography, flickr Creative Commons; Moon Waxing Crescent by John Spader (daspader), flickr Creative Commons; Full Moon by Nasa Goddard Photo and Video, flickr Creative Commons; **TheQuarters:** Weather Vane From Below by Tim Sheerman-Chase, flickr Creative Commons; Compass Rose by Margaret W. Carruthers, flickr Creative Commons; The Open Window by siegertmarc, flickr Creative Commons; Windows by JJ Losier, flickr Creative Commons; **TheElements:** Wiccan Five Elements1 by Nyo, Wikimedia Commons; Zywioly01 by Ratomir Wilkowski, Wikimedia Commons; **Air:** Burning Incense at Shaolin Temple by Kevin Poh, flickr Creative Commons; **Fire:** Sunrise With Bit of Spike by normanack, flickr Creative Commons; Fire Salamander by William Warby (wwarby), flickr Creative Commons; Lightning Storm by Benjamen Benson, flickr Creative Commons; **Water:** Florida Fighting Conch Shell by Trish Hartmann, flickr Creative Commons; Waterfall by Keith Roper, flickr Creative Commons; Drip Drop by Lizard10979, flickr Creative Commons; Welcome Back Moon by Jackie (Sister72), flickr Creative Commons; **Spirit:** Barred Spiral Galaxy NGC 6217 by Nasa Goddard Space Flight Center, flickr Creative Commons; Oak Maze Gill by Vik Nanda, flickr Creative Commons; Sider Web by Darren (estoril), flickr Creative Commons; **AltarRitualTools:** Museumsdorf by weisserstier, flickr Creative Commons; **Spells:** Aged Paper Texture by Essence of a Dream, flickr Creative Commons.

Herbs: Pot of Herbs by Tristan Ferne (tristanf), flickr Creative Commons; **DrumCircles:** Djembe Drums by ZSM, Wikimedia Commons; Ibiza Roda de Tambores by Rodrigo Sa, flickr Creative Commons; Drum Circle at the Dedication by moonlightclub, flickr Creative Commons; Matrimonio Etnia Bobo by Marco Fumasoni, flickr Creative Commons; Dancer Playing the Drums by Frank Kovalchek (Alaskan Dude), flickr Creative Commons; **Chants:** IMG 5284 by eyeliam, flickr Creative Commons; Si Ana Ay Buntis Na by Reuel Mark Delez (kamalayan), flickr Creative Commons; Temaristock Sunset by Temari 09, flickr Creative Commons **Seasons:** Crocuses and a Bee by Muffet, Wikimedia Commons; Kids Swimming at Hungry Mother by vastateparksstaff, flickr Creative Commons; Happy Thanksgiving by Faith Goble, flickr Creative Commons; Me Squirrel, You… by Dawn Huczek, flickr Creative Commons; May You Be Warm by belindah, flickr Creative Commons; **8Sabbats: Yule:** Star Sun Moon snow by Chris Baranski (cbb4104), flickr Creative Commons; **Imbolc:** Spring Arrives in Botanic Gardens by Cristian Bortes, flickr Creative Commons; **Ostara:** Stonehenge Spring Vernal Equinox 2013 by The Stonehenge Website, flickr Creative Commons; **Beltane:** The Maypole by April Killingsworth, flickr Creative Commons; **Litha:** Sun Woman by Frank Kovalchek, flickr Creative Commons; Midsummer Day 06 by Antti T Nissinen (V31S70), flickr Creative Commons; **Lughnassa:** Bales of Straw by Lars Kasper, flickr Creative Commons; Staff of Life by Robert Couse-Baker, flickr Creative Commons; **Mabon:** IMG 4617 Apple Harvest of 2010 by Johan Lange, flickr Creative Commons; IMG 2130 by Rebecca Smiles, flickr Creative Commons; **Numerology:** Mathrubhumi Kerala India Calendar by Jennifer Kumar, flickr Creative Commons; The Message #1 by Linda (jinterwas), flickr Creative Commons; **Alphabets:** Theban letters by Fuzzypeg, Wikimedia Commons; **Planets:** All planet photographs Mercury, Venus, Earth, Mars, Jupiter, Saturn, Uranus, Neptune, Pluto by Chris Meller, flickr Creative Commons; **Zodiac:** #49 Notebook by Ken Rosling (KaySeeArr), flickr, Creative Commons; **ChoosingMagickalName:** White Faced Scops Owl by Grahame Bentley, flickr Creative Commons; **SelfDedication:** Alone by Jon Clegg, flickr Creative Commons; Cloak By the River by Lucky Lynda, flickr Creative Commons; In Remembrance by Alosh Bennett, flickr Creative Commons; **InitiationIntoThePath:** Weird Ritual in the Park by Kate B. Harding, flickr Creative Commons; East Iceland's Pagan Priest by silkeybeto flickr Creative Commons; **ContinuingthePath:** Dalby City of Troy Turf Maze by Simon Garbutt (SiGarb), Wikimedia Commons; Harvest Moon by Steve Wilson (Loco Steve), flickr Creative Commons. **Collage2:** Spider Web by cybershotking, flickr Creative Commons; India Chennai Festival of Lamps 07 by McKay Savage, flickr Creative Commons; Runes and Rust by Sybil Liberty, Wikimedia Commons. Credit has been given to these photographs in accordance with Attribution License http://creativecommons.org/ licenses/by/2.0/legalcode and http://commons.wikimedia.org/wiki/Commons:Reusing_content_outside_Wikimedia. Photography not credited on this page is the author's own work and under copyright. **References:** Cunningham, Scott. *Wicca: A Guide for the Solitary Practitioner*. St. Paul: Llewellyn Publications, 1992. ISBN-10: 0875421180.; Gallagher, Ann-Marie. *The Wicca Bible: The Definitive Guide to Magic and the Craft*. New York: Sterling Publishing Co., Inc., 2005. ISBN-13: 978-1402730085.; Greenwood, Susan, and Airey, Raje. *The Complete Illustrated Encyclopedia of Witchcraft and Practical Magic*. London: Hermes House, 2008. ISBN-13: 978-1846810442.; O'Gaea, Ashleen. *The Family Wicca Book: The Craft for Parents and Children*. St. Paul: Llewellyn Publications, 1993. ISBN-10: 0875425917.; Serith, Ceisiwr. *The Pagan Family: Handing the Old Ways Down*. St. Paul: Llewellyn Publications, 1994. ISBN: 0875422101. ***Thank you to my family and friends for your support; Joy Burton for always sharing your light; Naropa fierce goddesses Beckett Coppola and Mehgan Fox. Most importantly, thank you to my damsels not in distress Brooke and Jessica Jr., my consort Trey, and our familiar Puggy. BB)O(

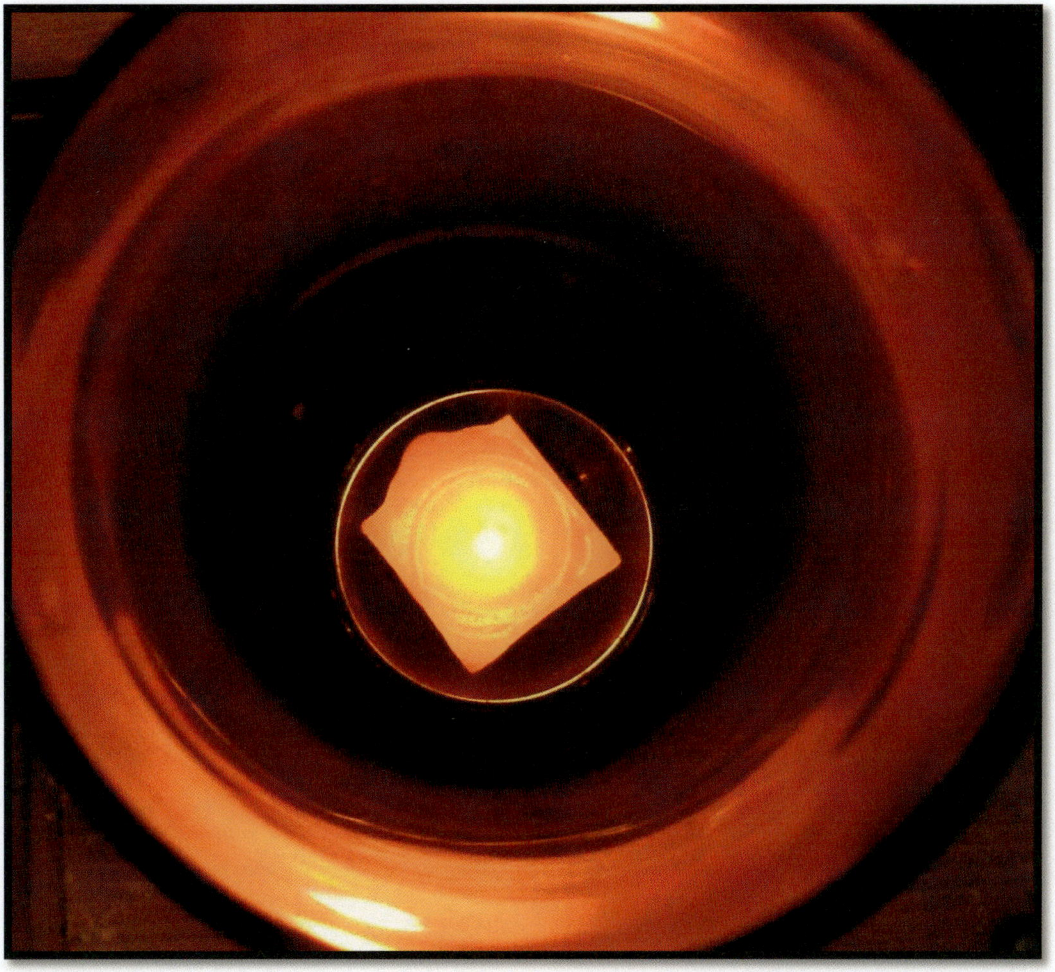

10368438R00053

Printed in Great Britain
by Amazon.co.uk, Ltd.,
Marston Gate.